THAT V WORD

Rock-Solid Foundations:

How Core Values Shape Your Life and Business

Dixie Maria Carlton

First published 2023 by Dixie Maria Carlton
©Copyright Dixie Maria Carlton 2023

Produced by Indie Experts

Apart from any fair dealing for the purpose of study, research or review, as permitted under the copyright act, no part of this book may be reproduced by any process without written permission of the author.

Every effort has been made to trace and acknowledge copyright material; should any infringement have occurred accidentally the author tends her apologies. Product or other trade names used herein may be trademarks of their respective owners. The author disclaims any and all rights on those marks.

Cover design: Daniela Catucci @Catucci Design
Edited by Geoff Taylor

ISBN: 978-1-7386102-1-1 Print
ISBN: 978-1-7386102-2-8 Digital

Disclaimer: Every effort has been made to ensure this book is as accurate and complete as possible, however there may be mistakes both typographical and in content. Therefore, this book should be used as a general guide and not as the ultimate source of information contained herein. The author and publisher shall not be liable or responsible to any person or entity with respect to any loss or damage caused or alleged to have been caused directly or indirectly by the information contained in this book.

Indie Experts Publishing & Author Services
www.indieexpertscoaching.com
New Zealand

*For Stacey and Hannah – my two favourite daughters.
I am so blessed by your presence in my family.*

Contents

Introduction..5

1 The V Word Conundrum..11
2 Self-Worth and Personal Value 19
3 Good old fashioned family values..23
4 We *give* value, but we *have* values......................................35
5 *Core* values 43
6 Your top core values...53
7 The needs component..61
8 That old 'Integrity' chestnut...67
9 Principles and virtues...79
10 Why we need to teach our kids about values 93
11 Relationship values 99
12 Company values 107
13 Displaying and living your brand values..........................117
14 Recruitment and company values.....................................123
15 Leadership and values..131
16 Summary...139

Resources and Tools...145
Acknowledgements..147
About Dixie Maria Carlton 149

Introduction

In the 'Olden Days' of horse drawn carts, town criers, and fighting the enemies with cross bows and hammers, we probably didn't think much about what made us all tick. If your neighbor was acting suspiciously like a witch, we might see them dunked to see if they'd float, and if the local butcher sold meat that had maggots cut out of it before being wrapped in a cloth to take home, you'd forgive him because that was simply how things were. Now, here we are in the 21st century and everything has a science, and overthinking is commonplace. We seek to understand each other in ways that our ancestors would have written off as witchcraft or lunacy and we have acronym-based labels for just about everything there is to put a label on. And every*one*.

However, the concept of having values, or principles has always existed. They were easier to dismiss in favor of status and wealth back in the day, because it mattered not whether the landed gentry on whose acreage your village dwelled upon was good or bad as he was king of your corner of the world, and that was that. We didn't elect people to positions of power and authority, we just accepted those who stepped into such positions were likely to be of either sound character, or sadly not, and adjusted our expectations accordingly.

While the values we have are in line with those once termed to be vices, principles, or 'a bad attitude' it is important that in this 21st century we do get a better understanding of these, because quite simply, they are at the root of all those other 'over thinking' based sciences.

I've long been fascinated by the intersection of how our values, core values, needs, personality types, and love languages make each of us uniquely beautifully special. In day to day living, this is hugely helpful to relationship building and of course personal satisfaction with decisions we make. In business, this same knowledge can mean the difference between a company that thrives, versus merely survives as it goes to the heart of our expectations around leadership. If leaders' and managers' values are unclear, they can easily be misaligned with a company's very purpose. Those who work under such mis-matched entities can easily end up disillusioned and frustrated by what they perceive as simply bad management.

Leaders who really are managers, and managers who are good or bad leaders might also take note of the difference between these roles, but further understanding core values will ensure that managers who are task oriented, versus leaders who are visionary can also better make sense of, and develop, their environments.

Over the last 20 plus years in my work as a specialist business coach I have developed these tools, and pondered deeply on each of these points I now share with you dear reader. It is my sincere desire that the information you find in the following pages helps in some small way at least to help you gain clarity about what drives you, inspires you, and how to best get your most important needs met. Because then you will be happier, and more satisfied through a level of self-awareness that will enable you to more easily set boundaries for yourself and manage your expectations of success. At the very least, I also hope you will share this wisdom with the children who come next, so that they too can better understand each other and those they must spend time with.

You might also wonder why I've included this book into the *Taboo Conversation* Series. The more I notice people talking about this topic and noting the apparent confusion around what values, versus core values are, and how they impact on our lives, I've come to see this as a topic that not only confuses, but also seems to be one that many like to take a stand on. Therefore, I see that this book might feel as though I'm correcting a number of those confused people, and that is something always treated with care and caution. However, I do believe that a better understanding of these can only lead to better communication, relationships, and consideration of each other worldwide.

Dixie

How to use this book

The first part is all about explaining value, values, and core values, as well as the needs we all have. This is relative to personal decision making, family and other relationships' care and development. The second part of this book is more focused on how values are applicable to work, company marketing, finding and developing great people to work with, and why it's important to align your values with your business.

There are access points to resources throughout the book, in particular downloadable worksheets on page

Part One

What values are and why the matter

1

The V Word Conundrum

In this age of pandemics, THAT V word could just as easily be Virus, or Vaccinations. Yes indeed, V words are generally hot topics right now. So why am I calling this book 'That V Word'? Well, I have noticed a growing number of people also talking about Leadership, or lack of it, and as part of that, any conversation about leadership also ventures into Values. And we all know that *values* are an overused, and greatly misunderstood term – or do we?

It turns out, that Value, Value*s*, and *Core* Values are greatly misunderstood, but that mostly we all think we know what they are, and the difference between these. The thing with that is, that for as long as we misunderstand what these are, the more we mess up what they really mean to us, and how we incorporate them into our lives.

If you ask most people about their values, you'll find they'll smile, and say, oh yes, I have values. I know mine are *Honestly,*

Integrity, Trust. Maybe *Respect* will also feature in their list. Yawn!

Seriously, I do mean: Yawn!

How can it be that so many of us have these exact same values? Especially when there are so many (I mean dozens) of other words that could be used. I believe it's a matter of most people wanting to be seen to be having the 'right' values. I mean, don't we all want to align ourselves with people like us – and aren't those values of Honesty and Integrity the best ones to have?

Well, what If I start by saying that Integrity is not a value?

I'm going to challenge a lot of your thinking on this in the pages to follow. I want to help you understand the difference between **value** – what we value, why we value things and people, and situations, and then how such a similar word **'values'** relates to who we are, how we function individually based on our individual values, and then how our core values are another level again. I also want you to understand the special ways you can use your values in things like your CVs, job applications, and even your online dating profiles, as well as in your business if you are self-employed.

If more businesspeople understood the difference between value, values, and core values, their brand values would be better able to act as a compass when it comes to their respective decision making about marketing, recruitment, and planning. You see, having values is important in any business, and for us as individuals. They serve like Jimminy Cricket to ensure that we stay true to who we are, even when we're faced with challenges. There is a saying that goes something like this: 'you only really know who someone is by how they react to the little things that come up'.

But let's not make this too complicated just yet. For starters, let's tackle what we think of as Value, and progress from there to the difference in what Value*s* are. It's almost a challenge of the English Language that these two V words are so close to each other in terms of how they are spelled.

The concept and meaning of VALUE

Just to be clear on a few points with this, I turned to Dr Google and went looking for all the ways these words are used. Here's what I found.

Value as a noun, according to dictionary.com means:

1. Relative worth, merit or importance – such as the value of an education or the value of a queen in a game of chess.
2. Monetary or material worth – as in trade
3. The worth of something in terms of the other things for which it can be exchanged.

4. Equivalent worth or return in money, material services etc – to give value for value received.

Value as a verb however is about considering what something is worth, its usefulness or importance. It's also about calculating or appraising assets.

Synonyms for VALUE included utility, cost, price, and prize.

Other words related to value included importance, profit, power, content, significance, purpose, benefit and amount. *So far, no mention of respect, honesty, or trust... see where we're going with this?* But here's where it gets interesting and probably a big part of why we're all so confused about the difference.

A value is stated as:

Both a principle standard or quality considered worthwhile and desirable,

and

As an assigned or calculated numerical quantity.

To use VALUE in a sentence, the online dictionary gave me these options:

'It's a crime that goes against all human **values** and norms'

And:

'With time this land had mounted to great **values** and the holders have been made well-to-do thereby'.

Where did this word even come from?

The old French word *Valior*, and from Latin *Valere* – both meaning to be worthy, strong.

Are you sharing my frustration yet with how hard it is to see the easy difference between these words?

Let's look at what other languages do:

English	Value	value<u>s</u>
Spanish	Valor	valores
Greek	Axia	axies
German	Wert	werte
Afrikaans	Waarde	waardes
Japanese	Kachi	kachi
Czech	Hodnota	hodnoty

No – not much help there – other languages don't really make a big distinction between the words Value and Value<u>s</u>.

However, I can see I'm going to have to change the title of this book for foreign translations.

What do we value and why?

We value people, friendships, our work. We value our children, grandparents, family, and in many instances, we value our things. That's why the insurance companies make so much money for their beautiful offices around the world. The value we place on stuff is what makes the world spin. We might value our youth – and therefore put value on cosmetics, dieting options, clothing, and things that make us look and feel good. We might place a sentimental value on precious things like our wedding rings, our photo albums, or other things that remind us of special events, people, or places.

But these are external things. **_We place a value on them_**. They are outside of ourselves.

For three years in my late forties, I was director in a company that bought and sold antiques. The specialty was jewelry but there were a host of other things exchanged too. I also got to see a lot of other types of businesses in this industry, like those who specialized in old coins, books, crockery, collectables, and yes, junk. *What's one man's junk is another man's treasure* was clearly obvious in this industry from my up-close perspective. The biggest lesson I learned from my three years in that business was that those things we place value on and insure, preserve, dust, and treasure, are quite simply just *things*. Things that others often fail to see the value of in the same way. So, *what* we value, *how* we value things, and *what is valuable* for some and not for others is worth remembering as we continue to explore the differences between Value, Values, and Core Values.

2

Self-Worth and Personal Value

Our personal worth, and those things about us which others may value in us, is a different thing again. What do you value in yourself? What are you grateful for?

The practice of daily gratitude is promoted by many coaches, and specialists who inspire peace and acceptance in our daily lives. Being grateful and *living in an attitude of gratitude* is said to help ensure the universe continues to bestow favor upon us as we focus on the good over the negatives in our lives.

Some ways to consider what is worthy of your *placing value on* might include:

Having great hair, long legs, good boobs, strong arms, a pretty/handsome face, a quick mind, the ability to make friends easily, confidence, a great sense of humor, nice kids, happy parents, healthy parents, healthy happy kids, good health for yourself.

Let's take that further and consider why these things might be of value – because you have to know why you value something for it to be meaningful. If you don't believe me, try standing in front of your best friend and justifying why you want to chop off your long hair, or why you need to keep paying your health insurance.

I value having:	Because:
Having great hair,	It keeps me warm, looks attractive, people compliment it
Long legs,	So that I can walk/run faster, look great in a skirt
Strong arms,	To hold my loved ones; to carry things
A pretty/handsome face,	To help me feel good about myself
A quick mind,	To help me get through life; to do the work I like to do
The ability to make friends easily,	To have good company, to not be lonely; to have someone to go to shows with
Confidence,	It's better than the alternative in most instances
A great sense of humor,	So that I can laugh at myself and others with grace and fun
Nice kids,	Because it's better than having horrid ones
Successful kids	So that they don't want to still live at home in their 30s
Happy parents,	So that we don't have big family dramas; so that we learn good habits
Healthy parents,	So that we don't need to center our lives around their health needs at this

	time of our lives; so they are happy too
Good personal health,	Because the alternative sucks!

Create your own list – what do you place value on about yourself and your current circumstances, and how does this play into your daily habit of being grateful. Because… would you be grateful for things that you don't value?

How would you treat things you value vs those things you don't value?

Chances are, when you have a clear understanding of the things you value *and why*, you will nurture and sustain those as best you can. For example, there's nothing like being reminded to value your teeth when ending up being told you have to sacrifice one or all due to a gum or tooth problem. So, if you value your teeth, you are more likely to invest in regular dental checks. If you value your hair, you're more likely to look after it, and invest in hair product, regular stylist appointments, and appreciate how it makes you look. If you value your parents' health, you are more likely to ensure they are looking after themselves and are able to continue to do so for as long as possible.

When it comes to being a good worker, or a valued employee, you might want to seriously consider your self-worth and the value you bring to the company you work for too. For example, do you have a great work ethic, skills, talents, and are you likely to be a good fit for the company you work with in regard to these things? Can you increase your value based on your skills and talents to increase your earning potential?

How can you increase your value to others?

3

Good old fashioned family values

What are they and why do we still talk about them this way?

Several well-known online dictionaries define "family values" as the following: "the moral and ethical principles traditionally upheld and passed on within a family, as **fidelity, honesty, truth, and faith.**" Now that sounds like something straight out of Little House on the Prairie, doesn't it? Or maybe the Waltons?

Families have changed dramatically in many ways since those good old days. And while we're talking Hollywood versions of these things, let's also remember that sex was never featured in any of those shows, and boys didn't cry either. While the idea of fidelity honesty, truth and faith are a lovely set of *ideals*, western society has evolved (not necessarily for better) in ways that makes some of these redundant values.

Let's look at the last 50 – 100 years and the differences that make these values seem so old fashioned in 2023.

Organised religion plays a lesser part in many western societies now, with agnostic, atheist, and spiritual all even finding their way onto census forms. So there goes faith (as it was first intended in this description). Fidelity, well, in homes where the divorce rates are significantly higher than

back in the post war era, it's now ok for mum or dad to have new partners, short term or long-term relationships beyond their marriages. The idea of fidelity may now have even been removed as a reason for divorce, in a no-fault legal sense, so fidelity as a nice ideal for many couples, is no longer guaranteed to make it to the top of the family values list.

Truth and honesty – well there we have two old fashioned family values that never really go out of style. Mums still hate it when their kids lie about homework, or what their siblings really did to contribute to the current drama, and isn't truth and honesty kind of the same thing?

When I hit up Dr Google for some more examples of family values for our modern times, I stumbled across one list that included things like:

- Creativity
- Fun

- Eating together
- Respect
- Hard work
- Responsibility
- Kindness

I thought to myself, there are some lovely ideals in there too. Eating together as an old-fashioned family value would never have even entered the minds of the Waltons - pass the black eyed peas thank you Jon-boy. They just did that as part of what life was about. You ate together, and complimented Mamma for the meal after you excused yourself from the table, and the girls did the dishes while the men sat on the porch and talked about what the sunset might mean for tomorrow's weather.

Eating together as a family value in the 2020s is kind of a sad value to have in such a list, simply because of what it says about our modern world and busy lifestyles. For a family to list this as one of their values is lovely. As is kindness, responsibility, and the others in this list. But how many families do you know who actually create a list, stick it on the fridge door, and honor those values?

When I was raising my sons, as a single parent, we discussed values, and house rules. We *all* had to honor these two values: Be honest with each other and respect each other. Trust and Respect were the only real rules, and they were adhered to. That meant that we all had to speak our truth, be honest about anything that happened (including if that meant admitting a wrongdoing or act of stupidity).

Respect was about ensuring that we didn't create a need for unnecessary worry for each other, so if we were going to be late home, we let each other know. If we were going to go from one place to another, we let each other know. If we were going to have to have a serious conversation about something that was wrong in any area of our lives, we chose our timing, didn't just throw the big bad thing on the table and leave the other(s) distraught over it, and we nurtured each other through the big stuff. This included when decisions were made about leaving home (for my kids), traveling overseas, career changes, relationship statuses, and selling the (then current) family home.

It also meant that we respected what each other owned in the house, and our own things. I have to say, delightfully, this put a major level of responsibility on both my sons around bringing home appropriate school notes, homework, and almost zero loss of clothing and property over the years.

That was easy – raising a small family with values as our guiding principles. We did have some others, such as kindness, responsibility, having fun, working hard and rewarding effort. But the Trust and Respect were the core values of our home.

Now this is where it gets tricky. You see I already dismissed the concept of honesty, trust, respect, and integrity in chapter one, as being values worth citing as your core values. And here too is where the confusion often remains in any discussion about the V words. So, let's take this to another level.

Let's say that Trust, Honesty, Truth, Respect are simply a given. Just like eating together as a family in the Waltons era was a given. These are so basic to the concept of being a 'good person' that we can in most instances assume these to be core values. Central to all the others. In that case, let's just leave them on the table, but accept that aside from narcissists and sociopaths, we *all* subscribe to the basic core values of Trust, Honesty, Truth and Respect.

However, the difference for some people is that these are discussed and understood as being values that have well descripted meanings for those people or their families.

As I was completing this book, I took time out to ask my two adult sons about their perspective of growing up with specific values in our family, and what they believed ours were. They both responded with a couple of different ones. One said, Fairness – and a sense of always doing the right thing, even if no one was there to see it. But they both said they felt our other family value was around independence. And we did all end up quite protective of that value in particular. Each has traveled well, forged their own unique and successful paths, and are outstanding young men. When we discussed all this together, they were in complete agreement about the four core values they then believed we had lived by for so many years – Honesty, Respect, Independence, and Fairness, and that these continue to be strong values for them. It was great to have that conversation given that I didn't really focus on the specifics of calling these our family values when they were young – we just all lived them and at times discussed them as rules of our home.

In a later chapter we'll look at how you can identify your other values and core values. For now, though, let's look at how you can make your own family values come into being as part of your household rules and make them become meaningful for all your family.

Exercise

Respect		Kindness		Education	
Care of elderly relatives		Eating together		Attending each other's events	
Truth		Play		Fun	
Loyalty		Fidelity		Affection	
Savings($)		Frugal		Generosity	
Healthy		Exercise		Nurturing	
Dreams		Responsibility		Work for rewards	
Independence		Discovery		Adventure	

You'll see I've left a couple of spare spaces for you to add something of your own.

Now take some time with your family to discuss each of these values and see what you can all agree on as being ones you will hold forth as your own family values. Circle these – get down to around 3-5 only.

Now write beside the ones you have elected, what these actually mean. How will you all work together to make these become meaningful for your family?

Here are some examples:

Care of elderly relatives	We will visit our grandparents regularly, and ensure they are looked after and looked out for in times of need. We will ensure our elderly relatives are included in our family in these ways.	Eating together	We will eat together at least 5 times each week – we will eat at the table, with no TV or Phones or interruptions at mealtimes. We will set a family tradition for our adult children that we gather weekly/monthly for a family mealtime.
Truth	We will commit to truth and honesty in our conversations, communications, and time together – even when the truth might not always be easy to say or hear.	Play	We will prioritize play in our holidays, in our home, and use play to learn and bond with each other.
Loyalty	We will be loyal to each other ahead of outside friendships, relationships, and opportunities.	Fidelity	As a couple we will be true and faithful to each other. Physically and emotionally.
Savings($)	We will always	Frugal	We will be a

	work to ensure we have reserve savings and will spend and invest carefully with consideration for each other's needs.		family of savers, so that we do not risk our livelihoods on frivolities.
Mutual Support	Whenever possible we will prioritize school plays, sports events, plays or whatever comes up, to be supportive of each other when things are happening. We will be each other's biggest fans.	Fun	Our holidays will be focused on fun, building fun memories, and we will use humor to support our communications whenever possible.
Affection	We will show affection for each other. We are a huggy family.	Generosity	We volunteer our time and goodwill to assist each other and those outside our family who need our assistance.

You might only have four or five for your family – these are just examples of how to make them work, so that everyone understands and agrees to them.

The thing about having recognized and discussed family values that you all agree on, means you have a compass for decision making. This extends to everything from family holiday planning, financial planning, and even how you commit to spending time together.

Decide what's most important and put those values and their respective *'and so that means…'* statement in a frame, somewhere easily seen and referred to throughout the years. When you have family meetings – also a good idea – then you have these to further guide the planning and communication around important matters.

If companies can have regular meetings to ensure everyone knows what is going on, what is being planned and even emergency planning and futureproofing, then why should your family not adhere to the same principles for important communication matters?

This really does work.

Try it.

Note: If your family has not gone down the path of having family meetings, you might want to try this as a starting point. Make it fun, put a note up on the fridge, check that it's a time and day that works for everyone, promise fun food, and for everyone to bring something to contribute to the conversation. You might want to write up a simple agenda – something like:

You're ALL Invited

SPENCER FAMILY GATHERING

Mum and Dad's Place

4PM: 20/01/2022

It's time for us to gather together on Sunday at 4pm around the table on the Deck, for the purposes of discussing:

Our next family holiday
Christmas – where and who's invited
Mum's 50th Birthday celebrations in April

PS – there will be apple cider, crackers, cheese, and popcorn served
If you want Chocolate, or prefer tea to Cider, please BYO.

No excuses – if you are part of this family, you are part of the conversation.
Pizzas ordered AFTER discussions ended – or by 5.30 – whichever comes first.

4

We *give* value, but we *have* value**s**

Value of something is what you or someone else gives it. As discussed earlier, we value things, situations, memories, opportunities, education, people treasure, property etc. But Value*s* are something we have.

The values we have are our internal drivers. Our values are those which make us who we are, and drive us to do things, try things, accept things, or walk away from things. They may be very different from our family values, or they may be very similar. They may be aligned with our partners or our best friends' values, or very different.

Let's explore what it means to *have* values

This table contains values you might have:						
tenderness	perceive	design	foster	spark	attractiveness	endeavour
compassion	discernment	imagination	helpfulness	stimulate	elegance	venture
touch	observe	inventiveness	facilitate	energize	refinement	quest
empathy	realize	ingenuity	improvement	encourage	loveliness	curiosity
responsiveness	knowing	originality	encourage	inspire	taste	Learning
supportive	aware	creative	nurture	create	grace	discovery

connection	sensuality	superiority	encouragement	emotiveness	prevalence	preparedness	honouring
unity	hedonistic	mastery	enthusiasm	energy flow	predominate	information	acceptance
nurturing	bliss	primacy	interest	sensitivity	triumph	sharing	devotion
family	touch	leadership	persuade	empathy	attainment	surety	passion
integration	gentle	sportsmanship	inspire	care	diligence	willingness	religious
kindness	sexual	winning	supportive	sympathy	achievement	ready	considerate

Needs are different to values

Needs are the things that also drive us in various directions but a need is a *need*. Like water, food, shelter, for most of us, we have a variety of needs and yet so often these can also be cited as values.

Let's say you believe one of your values is being part of a community. Well, I'm going to propose that being around other people is a need. A need to be with people, to share in events, celebrations, ideas and their implementation. But as a value, you might say instead you have a value of community spirit. Maybe you can take that further and say you have a value of contribution. A value that drives you to contribute – whether to a community or to people you are close to. The need for a community might be a wider group of people. And maybe you have a need to be linked with or closely associated with a tribe of some description, but that doesn't necessarily also mean you have a need to contribute. Contribution is a value. To contribute is a need. Just as Generosity is a value, but to be generous is a need.

A need to be right, is also not a value, it's a need. Righteousness might however be a value. Justice might be one of your values, in which case you might need fairness to be a big part of your life. For example, in that case you might really struggle to live in a place where bureaucratic bungling or corruption are rampant.

Sex might be something you need in your life, if you have a high libido, but the need for sex does not make it a value. However, sexuality could be a value. Another one is adventure. You might have a *value* that relates to risk, and therefore a *need* for adventure, or to be able to get your adrenaline up on a regular basis.

While writing this, I stumbled into a long conversation with a couple of Country Fire Association members in Australia – Firies who serve on the front line for everything from local accidents to major bush fires. We had a discussion about adrenaline and how much it is a feature of post-traumatic stress syndrome for so many people. Military and emergency services work on a basis of debriefing after service nowadays, but often these issues of PTSD are triggered long after the main event that might be at the root of an ongoing stress issue. For example, the bush fires of 2009 in Victoria, Black Saturday was a particularly challenging one for these two people. And they both managed to cope with that – and you could easily argue that as Firies, they had needs associated with community, and service, also values of contribution, and risk.

But one of them, Mo, mentioned that it was not until her own home was under direct threat from one of the bushfires that it all took on a totally different meaning. Then, while that was something that had to be managed and she was already in a good place to get the necessary debrief after that event, the adrenaline was raised to such high levels that they were physically affected by it for months after. Those effects included for one of them their ability to drink tea or coffee, or to tolerate the taste of certain foods. That's a PTSD issue – and not a *values* or *needs* issue. However, PTSD can affect your ability to have your needs met. Again, understanding what those are is easier to help with the process of dealing with how they are being impacted by trauma.

What does this have to do with values and needs?

People who need their adrenaline pushed as a regular thing in their lives may very well also have values of service, or not. Those who do might sign up for police, military, nursing, emergency care, coast guard or CFA work etc. But those who don't who also have the value of service, might instead have values relative to winning, or achievement, and their adrenaline needs are therefore better served by sport, competitions, performance, or mountaineering.

A value of discovery might drive someone to explore if they also have a need for exploration. But exploration is not a value – it's a need created by a value of discovery. A discovery value might also lead someone into the field of science. Again – a secondary value of risk would play into that career decision.

We have needs. We have values. And we have more than just one or two of these. It's the combination that makes us who we are.

5

Core values

Value is what we *give* to something that has meaning for us. Values are what we *have* inside of us that help drive our feelings and decisions about things in our lives. Let's take that one might step further and talk about our *Core* Values.

Our core values are those highest three, four or five that really cement the kind of people we are, how we react to things, what we stand for, who we associate with, and why. What we get out of situations, events, relationships also come down to our core values.

Just as the words suggest – our *core* values, are those most central to who we are.

For example:

Jenny works in a supermarket. She likes to turn up at work with a regular set of shifts set at the start of each week and generally the same people to work with. She likes a little variety as student workers come and go, but for the most part her work is predictable, stable, and the customers are of a reliable type who live in the area and are generally not transient types. Many are families and retired people. Jenny is able to get through her work with a minimum of supervision, and leave at the end of each day feeling good about her work. Her home life is generally predictable too – with the family living nearby, weekend lunches with her extended family and children, and band practice every Tuesday night. She travels with her long-term partner Brian to play jazz on long weekends at festivals around the region.

Jenny's values are Friendliness, Compassion, Compliance, and Service. She needs stability, routine, and a solid family. She also needs a sense of community and to be connected with stable, friendly people who appreciate her quiet lifestyle and relative lack of ambition. When the Covid 19 Pandemic started, Jenny was frustrated, scared and paid arguably far too much attention to the news. She also followed all the government guidelines about masks, quarantine and travel without question. She did this because her values of compassion were well and truly sparked by the chance of people dying and suffering from the virus. However, as time went by and the on and off again lockdowns started to affect her family gatherings and regular routines, her values of friendliness and compliance were severely impacted. Jenny started to notice her natural tendency towards friendly conversations with people at work were restricted by masks and general negativity. Not being able to actually see other smiles was far more challenging than she'd ever imagined. It got her down, and she spiraled into depression. Not being able to connect easily with her family further affected this. Not being able to meet for band practice – although sometimes they did all try to do this via Zoom for a while – added to her values being affected – this one was service. She was unable to serve her community with her music and be connected in friendship with her fellow band members.

Jenny is typical of the type of person who might appear on the surface to be relatively unaffected by such things as lockdowns – after all, supermarket staff were still able to work as essential services. But her values were still greatly impacted by the pandemic.

Jordan is a builder with a team of five others doing mostly renovations, and he runs a solid reliable business that he inherited from his dad, who still lends a hand on the tools occasionally. Jordan plays rugby league, and has a girlfriend, Sue, who plays representative level netball. She works as a legal aid assistant in a small law firm in the city. Jordan's Values are Reliability, Risk, Excellence, and Loyalty. He also needs to be in charge, to have money to spare, freedom to do his best work, and fun. Jordan managed his way through the pandemic lockdowns quite well because he mostly focused his work on renovations. His customers were loyal because they recognized his (values based) reputation for excellence and reliability, and he was also able to continue to work through with his team.

As the second and third lockdowns came though, Jordan's ability to guarantee completion times of jobs was hindered and his values of Reliability and Excellence were challenged. He was still able to work but being finished on time meant a lot to him. He also had enough money in reserve to retain his team who also were loyal, as were his clients. But the freedom to get his work done how he liked to and deliver on his brand promises of excellence and reliability were what kept him awake at night. He knew he had it better than some of his colleagues, but still could not resign himself to underwhelming his clients, even though so many factors were out of his control.

Sue, whose values were Diligence, Communication, and Sensitivity was also affected by the lockdowns but in completely different ways. Her law firm required a work from home rule, and she initially embraced this and enjoyed simply checking in with her manager by Zoom each morning and afternoon. However, her manager put a lot of their current projects on hold which compromised Sue's value of Diligence. She liked to start something and see it through. That was her way and stopping short of completion was very hard for her to accept. Zoom meetings at the start of each day also meant that Sue was unable to interact with those she worked with and her need for clear communication and feedback was not being met. Sue also needed to have goals to meet and to be stretched in her ability to step up and exceed expectations in her work. That was part of her core value of diligence. Having her work essentially pared back to basics caused her to second guess her value to the company.

You see, when we look at people like Sue, Jordan, and Jenny, it's easy to see how having your values can relate to the needs you have, and how when your needs are not met and your values are compromised, your feeling of being out of alignment with your environment, or with others makes you feel like you're out of step with the world in general.

One of my personal core values is Freedom. I crave it in such a way that any kind of clipping of my figurative wings makes me feel physically very uncomfortable. The idea that I may not just jump in my car and visit someone, go somewhere, or be free makes me agitated. Even if only a little bit, that agitation affects my concentration, and my ability to be warm and friendly about being stuck. As an aspect of my Core value of Freedom, I would never volunteer to travel to a country where I could get arrested for something I had no control over or risk my freedom in any way. The idea of doing a 14 day hotel quarantine made me feel nauseous (which was required for me to return to New Zealand in late 2021) and I need flexibility in my work and lifestyle generally. I even hate to have to wake up to an alarm, preferring to discipline myself and have the freedom to wake naturally. In short, I hate being hemmed in in any way, and would make a lousy factory employee who had to stand in one place doing the same things eternally. That's my idea of hell.

Freedom is arguably a pretty popular value. Lots of people will recognize this as a value and for those of us who have it as one of our core values, this means we are guided by this deeply and meaningfully. But you can have more than just a couple of values. Yes, you might have 3-5 CORE values, but you might also have a handful more. For example, Your Core Values are the ones you can't really ignore or live without. Some of your others might be simply easier to compromise on at least for a short time.

Let's explore the difference between General Values and Core Values.

You can download a Values and Needs Analysis Grid at:

www.dixiecarlton.com/Values-Resources

or create your own version to use in the following exercises.

Values List					
Endeavour	Venture	Quest	Curiosity	Learning	Discovery
Attractiveness	Elegance	Refinement	Loveliness	Taste	Grace
Spark	Stimulate	Energize	Encourage	Inspire	Create
Foster	Helpfulness	Facilitate	Improvement	Encourage	Nurture
Design	Imagination	Inventiveness	Ingenuity	Originality	Creative
Perceive	Discernment	Observe	Realize	Knowing	Aware
Tenderness	Compassion	Touch	Empathy	Responsiveness	Supportive
Honouring	Acceptance	Devotion	Passion	Religious	Considerate
Preparedness	Information	Sharing	Surety	Willingness	Ready
Prevalence	Predominate	Triumph	Attainment	Diligence	Achievement
Emotiveness	Energy Flow	Sensitivity	Empathy	Care	Sympathy
Encouragement	Enthusiasm	Interest	Persuade	Inspire	Supportive
Superiority	Mastery	Primacy	Leadership	Sportsmanship	Winning
Sensuality	Hedonistic	Bliss	Touch	Gentle	Sexual
Connection	Unity	Nurturing	Family	Integration	Kindness

Needs List

To Experiment	Adventure	Speculate	Danger	To Gamble	Discovery
Beauty	Be Attractive	Magnificence	Gloriousness	Radiance	Grace
Spark	Stimulate	Energize	Encourage	Inspire	Create
To Move Forward	Touch	To Coach	To Turn On	To Alter	To Produce
To Serve	To Strengthen	To Grant/Endow	To Assist	To Augment	To Improve
To Plan	To Assemble	To Make Stuff	To Inspire	To Build	To Complete
To Uncover	To Distinguish	To Detect/ Investigate	To Learn	To Share	To Identify
To Percieve	To Support	To Respond	Be Present	Be Compassionate	To Empathize
Be Enlightened	To Be Awake	Be Accepting	Acceptance	Be Holy	Be Peaceful
To Enlighten	To Edify	To Explain	To Uplift	To Instruct	To Educate
To Win Over	To Attract	Perfection	To Score	To Aquire	To Persuade
To Experience	In Touch With	Be With Others	Sensations	To Feel Good	To Be High
To Govern	To Model	To Influence	To Inspire	To Rule	To Guide
Sensuality	To Arouse	Be Aroused	Be Joyful	Be Gentle	Appreciation
Connection	Be Adept	Pre-eminence	To Dominate Field	To Out-do	Be Expert
Encouragement	Have Fun	Be Safe	Feel Secure	Be Risk-averse	Have Money

Use this one, download one, or create your own.

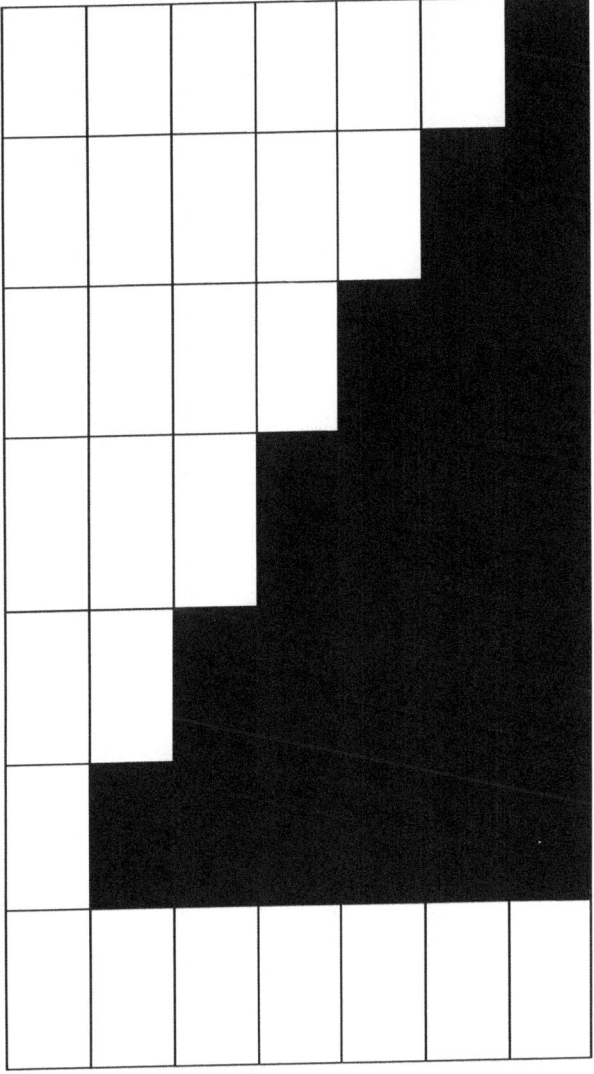

6

Your top core values

Knowing what your values are, and that there is a hierarchy of these helps to make sense of what integrity is all about. But first you need to identify what your overall values are, then narrow down to what your top 3-5 CORE values are.

Now let's identify YOUR values, your Needs, and Your CORE Values.

On pages 42 and 43 you'll find a list of Values and Needs you might have – starting with the VALUES list, identify up to 10 that you feel are ones you resonate with. Write these down on a piece of paper. You'll also find a link to download these templates on page 133.

When you have identified 6-10 or so values from the list above that resonate with you, narrow down this list to six, or maybe eight if you're really stuck. Then list them across and down the grid as indicated here.

List them across and down in the same order.

VALUES:	Prevalence	Mastery	Knowledge	Helpfulness	Pleasure	Risk
Prevalence						
Mastery						
Knowledge						
Helpfulness						
Pleasure						
Risk						

Now count each one against the other and decide which means more to you. Try not to overthink it, *and having someone else to walk you through it also helps prevent the overthinking.* Just tune into your gut feeling as much as possible and you'll quickly identify your priority options. But be warned, this might look really easy, but it's often a lot harder than it may appear to be.

VALUES:	Prevalence	Mastery	Knowledge	Helpfulness	Pleasure	Risk
Prevalence		Mastery	Prevalence	Helpfulness	Prevalence	Risk
Mastery			Knowledge	Helpfulness	Mastery	Mastery
Knowledge				Knowledge	Knowledge	Risk
Helpfulness					Helpfulness	Helpfulness
Pleasure						Risk
Risk						
Totals each	2	1	3	4	0	3

The Results

In this instance the outcomes are as indicated by how many times each was featured in the overall list:

- Helpfulness 4
- Knowledge 3
- Risk 3
- Prevalence 2
- Mastery 1
- Pleasure 0

Don't be surprised if one or two of these come out right at the bottom of your new list, and in some cases (in this instance Pleasure) don't rate at all. Remember this is still developed from a list of maybe 8 or 10 you initially worked from. This is essentially about pitting each value against all the others to see which ones resonate most strongly with you. I've done this exercise with hundreds of people now, and have never found someone not able to select their strongest values.

Take a fresh sheet of paper and number them (the top 4-5) in their new order.

Value:	Which means that/I live this through:	?
Helpfulness	I'll go out of my way to help others in need – even if it's inconvenient at times.	
Risk	I'm not risk averse – a little edge is well within my comfort range, and I'm happy to explore how far that goes.	
Knowledge	I commit myself to lifetime learning and expanding my knowledge, and my pursuit of knowledge will be something I'll always invest in with time, money, and a willingness to learn and share.	
Prevalence	I like to do things that ensure I am noticed and applauded when I achieve great things.	
Mastery	I commit myself to doing things well – completion and command of what I undertake to learn and develop skills in.	

When you have gone through this exercise and you are content that you have identified your top 3-5 *core* values, sit with this for a while, and continue to develop the 'this means that:' in the middle column. *Ignore the third column <u>for now</u>.*

Your Top Core Values

Those that you found were the more numerous against those that were not (in this case *Helpfulness* vs *Mastery* and *Pleasure*) will be what you can comfortably consider as your CORE values going forward. It's highly unlikely these will change over time, but you might at some point add one of your lesser ones into the top mix. For example, you may find that Mastery becomes a more important value to you depending on circumstances and maturity changes in your life.

The ones you chose that sit below this, (and feel free to extend this grid to actually measure out all 10 values you choose to see what order they fall into) are still part of your fundamental values to live by, but your primary or core ones are likely the ones you can't compromise on.

For example:

Using our example set above, you may also have had (in your initial selection of 10, which you then reduced to the six entered in your grid) Compassion, Grace, Acceptance and Nurturing. So, your other values would be:

1. **Helpfulness**
2. **Risk**
3. **Knowledge**
4. **Prevalence**
5. Mastery

6. Pleasure
7. Compassion
8. Grace
9. Acceptance
10. Nurturing

You are not limited to only 10, and you might end up deciding you're happy with just eight. It doesn't matter – this is personal to you.

Let's say your value as it relates to compassion means that you are by nature drawn to be compassionate, and there's some nurturing and helpfulness in there too. So maybe you would make a great nurse. Now let's say that you are faced with a situation where you are having to decide between compassion for someone, versus helpfulness for someone else. There's a clash in your mind – do you attend the funeral of a good friend's mother to honor your value of compassion, or do you help the other friend who really needs to see a specialist and her babysitter let her down at the last minute. It's likely your helpfulness (core) value will override your compassionate one, although both are called into play.

Another example might be that you are building a new home, and your builder calls to say you have two options – the beautiful new copper tiles that might make the difference between a house that gets featured in Home and Garden

Magazine, and therefore adds additional perceived value to it, but there's a high risk in using them because they are new to the market and you can't get any guarantee beyond five years for their durability. Your (core) value of risk is likely to override the other values of pleasure and grace simply because you're okay with the risk that it might not work out. But if you had a core value of security and were therefore risk averse then you wouldn't even have that conversation with your builder.

7

The needs component

Before we return to the final part of understanding your core values, you also need to identify your primary needs, so we can put it all together. So, let's now focus on doing that.

On page 43 you'll find the list of Needs, please select 6-10 that you feel resonate with you, and then narrow them down to around Six, to put into an analysis grid.

Go through the same process of identifying around 10 needs and then narrow them down to a top six. List them on your grid as per this example:

NEEDS:	To Improve	To Serve	Make Stuff	Perfection	Sex	Appreciation
To Improve		Serve	Make stuff	Improve	Sex	Appreciation
To Serve			Make stuff	Serve	Serve	Serve
Make Stuff				Make stuff	Make Stuff	Appreciation
Perfection					Sex	Appreciation
Sex						Appreciation
Appreciation						
Totals each	1	4	3	0	2	5

Your list of Needs:
- Appreciation 5
- To Serve   4
- To Make Stuff 3

- Sex 2
- To Improve 1
- Perfection 0

In order of importance: Appreciation, to Serve, to make stuff, Sex, to Improve.

So according to this example, you really need appreciation, and then to serve and to make stuff followed by the need for sex and to improve, but you discover that perfection is in reality a lot less important than you might have thought.

Most of us will go well out of our way to have our fundamental needs met.

This is not just about Maslow's hierarchy of needs which is classified into Self Actualization, Esteem, Love and Belonging, Safety and Physiological. This centers more around the top of the pyramid, into the area of self-actualization. What we *need* to have or do, to feel like we're having a good day.

In this example, the person who has this combination might find that baking a birthday cake that is better than the one they did last time – especially for someone who really does appreciate that effort - is going to feel pretty darned good about making that effort.

Where does this Needs list fit with our Values and Core Values lists?

In the table below, there is a third column. Some of the things in this Needs list relate to the Values list – but not all. For example, you could argue that the need to serve, and have appreciation is relative to the value of helpfulness. To make stuff and improvement could be tied to knowledge and mastery. But here's where I believe Values often hold more sway over our decision making than our Needs do.

If you have a Core value of *Helpfulness* you might also have a NEED that relates to that value that in this example simply accentuates how they fit together. In this instance a *Need to be Appreciated* for being helpful. Some people might have a value of helpfulness, but not need to be recognized for what they do.

Value:	Which means that:	Associated Need:
Helpfulness	I'll go out of my way to help others in need, even anticipating their needs so I can offer to be helpful.	But I need to be recognized and appreciated for my efforts.
Risk	I'm not risk averse – a little edge is well within my comfort range, and I'm happy to explore how far that goes.	I need to feel stimulated by the thrill of taking chances sometimes.
Knowledge	I commit myself to lifetime learning and expanding my knowledge, and my pursuit of knowledge will be something I'll always invest in with time, money, and a willingness to learn and share.	I need to know things and to learn, share, teach what I discover through my learning.
Prevalence	I like to do things that ensure I am noticed and applauded when I achieve great things.	I need the recognition that comes with being on top of my game.
Mastery	I commit myself to doing things well – completion and command of what I undertake to learn and develop skills in.	I need to finish things I start, and not doing things in a half-hearted way.

Can you see how this person might have these additional needs that don't necessarily have a close association with their values, but are somewhat of a fit in some areas? And that some of this person's needs are quite separate indeed?

Needs:

Appreciation | To Serve | Sex | To Make Stuff
To Improve | Perfection

When you marry up your core values and general values against your core needs and general needs, you get a much clearer picture of what is going to make you happy, and how well you'll be aligned with decisions. You'll more clearly understand when you are out of integrity with those values and needs from external influences.

8

That old 'Integrity' chestnut

Trust, Respect, Honesty, and of course Integrity. As stated earlier, these are the commonly stated values most people think of when asked about the concept. While I support that Trust, Respect and Honesty are indeed values, and high-ranking ones too, as now explained in the first few chapters, they are the 'assumed or given' values. However, Integrity is not a value. I know that might not sit well with a lot of people.

Just to recap:
- We have several values, and 3-5 CORE values that sit above the rest.
- We all have a different combination of values, core values, and needs, this is what makes each of us unique.
- Our values have some correspondence to some of our needs, but our needs may also be separate to our values.

- We *give* value to things/people/circumstances, but we *have* values.
- We can increase our perceived value to those whom we serve or associate with.
- Our core values will likely not ever change – they are part of who we are at our deepest levels.

When we are not getting our needs met, we feel grumpy, hard done by, or a fear of missing out might arise. The stronger the need for something, the more that level of negative feeling might plague us until we either get what we feel we need, or we find some way to let go of that specific need.

When we are out of alignment with our values, however, we feel 'odd'. Oddly out of step with whatever it is, or anxious about the status quo. We might find that the situation plays over and over in our minds as we try to make sense of it. When something doesn't make sense according to our values and beliefs, then we toss and turn with the status quo even more. Finally, if the issue is unresolved, we either park it away and stew on it quietly in the midnight hours of wakefulness, or we do our best to stomp down on that feeling of something not being quite right.

It's that feeling of it not being quite right that is what we call being out of integrity. Not being aligned with the thing –

having it rub against the hairs on the back of our necks even. Being out of integrity is quite simply having one of our values compromised. And it might not even be obvious to us for a while. In fact, sometimes a lack of integrity we notice in something we're personally responsible for might just feel like an undetermined 'itch in the brain' for a while until we get the chance to take it out and evaluate it.

For example. If you have values that relate to being sensitive, compassionate or nurturing, and someone cuts you off at the queue for the checkout, and it's a long queue, you might feel particularly frustrated by their actions and all feelings of compassion fly out the window, regardless of how tired that heavily pregnant woman looks. You still have had a hard day too and she pushed in, so you give her a snarly look, and mutter something under your breath – but you really don't feel good about it and it bothers you for hours. You get home, have your dinner, and reflect on how utterly exhausted she might have been, not to mention uncomfortable and very hormonal, but you made her hard day even worse. You might think it's just a case of the guilts, but really this is you having acted out of integrity with the compassionate caring kind person you usually are.

Let's say you worked really hard on a project at work, delivered the presentation to your boss and the client, having gone the extra distance and been extremely thorough and helpful (because diligence and helpfulness are part of your values), but they rushed you through the end, and didn't really appreciate your efforts, and left you hanging on an answer for the deal. This makes your values feel compromised because they didn't have those same values – there was a total mismatch. Your boss always puts you down because of your thoroughness whereas he's impatient and rash, and the client was lacking in values around mastery or excellence so really did not appreciate your time – so they made you feel anxious and subservient to their leadership related values. This is a clear mismatch of values.

Simply put, when your values are out of alignment with something or someone it's hard to 'be in integrity'.

Integrity is not a value you have, it's a state of being in alignment (or not) with your values.

That's not to say you can't commit to being in integrity. Many people and companies do and say this is part of what they are and who they are in their personal or commercial branding. But to be in integrity, you really must know what those values are. If someone promotes that they will operate with integrity that should mean they are saying they will be honest, trustworthy and respectful – the assumptive values. Stating they will do this as just saying they work with integrity is kind of like a double statement of the bleeding obvious.

Let's consider a Tech company.

We'll call this company Andy's Apps - AA for short. AA have been operating for around eight years and sell software to accounting firms. They have 20 employees, of whom eight are working in support and four are in development. The rest of the crew are in management and sales. Their company values are based closely on the agreed values of the three senior managers/owners, and are listed in their company documents as follows:

AAs is all about Resourcefulness, Helpfulness, and Communication. That means we work hard to ensure our clients have excellent tools and well-developed resources, developed with clear communication and feedback to help us all achieve more. Our helpdesk is open 24/7 and if we can't work out a problem we'll keep researching until we can.

AA also has just lost three key people from the development and support teams and replaced them with temps while they go through a recruitment process. Unfortunately, one of the temps is a bit loose with their promises and doesn't understand the company value of Helpfulness either. They didn't communicate their situation properly to a frustrated client and that client has now threatened to stop their contract. In a nutshell the client feels that the company is out of integrity, having put someone not up to the task to be in the support role, didn't support that person or check on them, and didn't communicate efficiently with the temp - or with them either - to resolve the issue in a helpful, resourceful, or efficient manner.

It's what you do even when no one can see you

As we've already discussed, you have values. You can have integrity. You can't GIVE it.

You can *have* integrity. You can *be 'in'* integrity. You can *act with* integrity. In that respect, it's easy to see why people mix it up as being another value. But it's such a core value that it goes much deeper than being listed as 'just another value'. I believe it sits in a whole class of its own.

Integrity is about doing what's right even when you are the only person who might even know about it. When there's no one there to see you pick up the other persons dropped $20 note, and you stop them to give it back to them. When no one else might stop to ensure that child you see running along the street is safe, or that tempting option to walk out of a restaurant without paying presents itself, your decision to 'do the right thing' is what being in integrity is all about.

When you *act with integrity* about something, it brings into play the values of honesty, trust, and respect all at the same time, and it's that Jiminy Cricket moment that chirps insistently at you from the good wee angel sitting on your shoulder, that is far louder and more obnoxious than the horny mischievous little devil trying to get you to push the boundaries between good and bad on the other shoulder.

When someone you are with has a different set of values than you have, it might not matter if one of you is all about *freedom, helpfulness and creativity*, and the other has core values of *perfectionism mastery and compassion*, integrity is not going to be part of the debate about doing the right thing or not – because that is a whole different issue.

But here is where it gets interesting...

When your own values are compromised – it brings up the

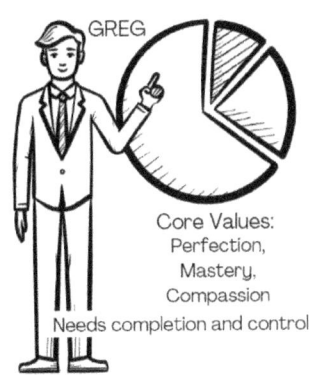

same feelings of being out of integrity and that's very hard to live with.

Let's take those two examples just given – one person – let's call him Fred, has core values of freedom, helpfulness, creativity and his boss, Greg, has core values of perfectionism mastery and compassion. Greg wants Fred to compromise on his **value** *of Creativity* in order to achieve a level of *perfectionism he* **needs** to be satisfied and happy with a project. Fred's core value of freedom (and need to be unrestricted) and creativity is unlikely to be able to step up to the required level of perfectionism and mastery that are Fred's core values. There's a complete mismatch of values, and both are going to feel out of sorts about compromising their core values to help meet the other's needs. Fred having another core value of helpfulness means he's likely to want to do everything he can to help Greg to achieve what he is aiming for, and Greg's other core value of compassion means he's going to really struggle to push Greg to his limits of frustration over this, but at the end of the day, each man is going to feel compromised over the project because their values are being pushed out so far.

Being out of integrity is the stuff that keeps you awake at night.

Let's look at another example:

Christy has a set of core values that are Sharing, Diligence, and Accomplishment, and her daughter-in-law Judy's core values are Improvement, Passion, and Communication. Christy likes to work things out and will diligently see things through to the bitter end once she takes on a project or new hobby. For her, getting close to her daughter-in-law represents an opportunity to teach her all about one of her favorite hobbies, and that's needlework. She has beautiful handmade quilts in all the bedrooms and gives one to Judy as a gift, along with an invitation to learn the craft and join her quilting group. Judy loves to see things improved and her own passion lies in the

area of design and decorating. The quilt idea is nice but not really in keeping with her current passion for modern décor, and so she puts the quilt on the spare bed and declines to learn the craft herself because she sees it as a frustrating and slow way to make something she could more easily buy in a more modern style for her home. Christy tries to explain her feelings on the matter – and really wants Judy to understand her point of view. Judy is busy and really can't see the problem - after all in her mind it's not like she 'just folded up the gift and relegated it to the linen cupboard, she put it in the guest bedroom for goodness sake!'

The ensuing fall-out centers on the mis-matched values of Sharing and Communication. Judy doesn't have the same values around sharing at all and fails to understand her mother-in-law's views on sharing as being one of the ways she wanted to get closer. Christy doesn't understand that her daughter-in-law's attempts to explain away her point of view are just as relevant and so Judy feels unheard and misunderstood for her efforts to discuss this and try to find a pathway to understanding why the big change in attitude.

The result is that Christy feels her daughter-in-law is unappreciative of her workmanship and her efforts to get close and Judy feels that her mother-in-law is sulky and uncompromising because she won't talk about the issue or meet her in the middle.

- If you have a core value of communication and someone else with whom you are supposed to be forming a relationship does not, then finding a way to understand each other is significantly harder.

- If you have a core value around sharing, and the other person does not – then one of you might end up feeling the other is selfish, while the other feels that too much is being thrust upon them.
- If you have a value of compassion and the other person does not, then one of you is going to feel put out about the other being uncaring and lacking empathy.

If you know your own core values, and you know what your needs are in relation to those values, then finding a way to get those values aligned with those you have relationships with is a lot easier.

A mismatch of values also easily brings about judgement between people. In many instances, we default to judging those who do not share the same values as we do, because we simply don't understand what drives them.

Which bring us to how it works – or not – when we have to manage our Brand values and employees, which is coming up in Chapter 11.

9

Principles and virtues

Often people seem confused by the concept of integrity when it comes to talking about Values. You'll frequently hear people say that Integrity is one of the core values. I don't believe it really is. In contemplating this chapter, I did some extra research into the general perception of what integrity means, and I really like this description on Wikipedia.

> *"Integrity is the practice of being honest and **showing a consistent and uncompromising adherence to** strong moral and ethical **principles and values**. In ethics, integrity is regarded as the honesty and truthfulness of accuracy. (And I really love this bit) Integrity can stand in opposition to hypocrisy."*

Breaking this down, it's clear that integrity is not a value of itself, but the willingness to show adherence to your principles and values. Arguably that might even be not so much strongly and ethical ones. For example: if your values are Information and Discovery, and you're a spy, (but a really good one) and you're working for the side you really feel is the best team, then maybe you could justify your values of Information and Discovery trump your values around Honesty or Security, Fairness or Justice. But the point is, standing strongly in line with your values and principles are what being in integrity is.

An Example based on Covid Mandating

As I write this chapter, there are many protests going on in New Zealand and Australia about individual rights to choose to be vaccinated for Covid 19 or not. As part of this mandating and pushing through of critical laws to give politicians increasing amounts of control, this personally triggers my own core value of Freedom. My core values as stated earlier are Freedom, Communication, Curiosity, and Helpfulness. For me to stand aside and do nothing at all to stand up against a democratic right of Freedom for myself and those around me, would mean my being out of integrity in terms of this particular value.

To do nothing but murmur quietly and sit on my hands in dull acceptance of something that does not satisfy my **Need for** *Flexibility* and my **Core Value** *of Freedom* would make me toss and turn at night and stress and worry over it. Because to do nothing did not allow me to practice a consistent and uncompromising adherence to a strongly felt moral and ethical principle and set of values. So I joined my first ever protest event.

People who protest, who march, and prevail over the ideology of the greater good do so because their core values at some level dictate they must. People who don't are not necessarily benign in their thinking about those causes, but have different values that they must also honor in their own ways.

Let's look at another example:

If you consider the reason for the protests about Freedom going on at the moment are also triggered by many people's need to debate the safety of the vaccinations, those people may have values around security, or discovery, justice, fairness, or information. They may be honoring their values by doing a lot of research about the vaccinations, and sharing their knowledge, protesting their feelings about justice in being forced to have a vaccination they don't believe in, because that allows them to stand in integrity around their own feelings on the matter.

That's just examples based on some current events. Looking further, someone who has a value of beauty or elegance, would be far less likely to destroy a work of art, than someone with a core value of creativity. The person with the core value of beauty would likely feel the utmost levels of guilt and that they had betrayed that value (i.e. been out of integrity with it) whereas the person with the creativity value might destroy a thing of beauty if that meant they could recreate it in a (to them) more meaningful way.

Being out of Integrity is often something you feel first in your gut. Your other brain – the stomach – will tighten, a slight sensation of anxiety will develop and grow, until eventually a whole chorus of Jiminy Crickets start yelling in your ear that something is just not right.

This is also about honesty. First with yourself.

If you try and lie to yourself about something that goes against your values or puts you in that uncomfortable feeling of something not being quite right, you'll eventually figure out that your lack of honesty with yourself is far more personally damaging than being honest, first with yourself, and then if someone else is involved, then also with them. This is true of relationships, just as much as with things like stealing, or other kinds of dishonesty.

If you were walking down the street, and found a wallet, with $100 in it. Or better yet, around $100 all made up in lose notes, so it wasn't really immediately clear just how much there was – but it looked like plenty. What would you do?

Let's say you were homeless, starving, or lost, and really needed to 'borrow' $10 before handing it in. Would you? Might you justify your actions and leave an IOU note? Then what – hope that they consider the 'borrowing' to be entirely justified – after all they may have given a finder's reward anyway... right?

How would you continue to feel about that over time?

I've known some people still feel guilty about seemingly mundane things such as this for many years. And others who justified their actions in countless ways so that it stopped bothering them. In one instance I heard a friend recount a story where they did 'just borrow' something that never got returned, and years later found out that the seemingly small missing item had caused a major long-term rift in a friendship.

Integrity is about doing what's right for you to feel good about having done the right thing by your own standards, as dictated by your own core values, even when no one else is looking.

Do Narcissists have Values?

This brings up the interesting question of Narcissists and Values. Some might argue that a narcissist might not actually have values at all. I'm not a psychologist and I'm not well researched on that complex issue. However, some of the many papers I've read in my delving into this topic tell me that yes, Narcissists certainly do have them.

A narcissist might have any of these values – risk, influence, accomplishment, excellence, pleasure, contribution, leadership or others. However, they may also *lack* a few additional aspects to their needs list, such as loyalty, honesty, respect. These are usually overridden by their needs for Control, Self-importance, and Appearance.

Narcissists might typically be known for their lack of respect, disloyalty and even honesty. They have a great need to be the center of their own universe and lack empathy to help themselves see their own behaviour in relation to others in their orbit. So, for a narcissist, being out of integrity is akin to having their needs be more important than their values, and those needs not being met sufficiently which makes them feel the same way a non-narcissist feels when they are out of integrity.

That other V Word: Virtues

If Value and Values are a little confusing, then let's go for broke and add the other big V word in, and talk about Virtues. I remember as a child my parent's constantly telling me that 'patience was a virtue'. Ok thanks, but I don't really think making me wait till after breakfast to have my presents on my birthday is fair, and what's a virtue anyway.? It was never really explained to me at the time, and in writing this book I decided first to not add this chapter in, and then realized it would not be complete at all without this next part. Afterall, this book is mostly about Values and Needs, because that's an area I work mostly in with my clients.

Let's dial it back a bit and ensure we all know exactly what the difference is. With a disclaimer however, that *this* V word seems to also be a little confusing and fraught with misunderstandings.

First I decided to consult with Dr Google and then www.dictionary.com to ensure I could explain it properly. Sadly, this left me feeling even more frustrated about the English language, as there were no less than 7 different nouns for the word Virtue.

1. moral excellence; goodness; righteousness.
2. conformity of one's life and conduct to moral and ethical principles; uprightness; rectitude.
3. chastity; virginity: *to lose one's virtue.*
4. a particular moral excellence.:
5. a good or admirable quality or property: *the virtue of knowing one's weaknesses.*
6. effective force; power or potency: *a charm with the virtue of removing warts.*
7. **virtues,** an order of angels.

Note that the last one is actually virtues, but on checking, found that the meaning for this is:

The fifth of the nine orders into which the angels are traditionally divided in medieval angelology.

One can be virtuous – which really just makes me think of chaste virginal lasses from the last few centuries in Europe who feature in stories by the Bronte sisters and anything by Jane Austen.

When young Benjamin Franklin, of publishing, writing, inventing and presidential fame from the USA was a strapping young 20 year old man, setting out to begin his adult life, he decided to write up a set of virtues to live by and these are often referred to by anyone seeking to explain the concept of character.

He is quoted as saying:

"It was about this time I conceived the bold and arduous project of arriving at moral perfection. I wished to live without committing any fault at any time; I would conquer all that either natural inclination, custom, or company might lead me into."

Arguably it is true that most of these are just as relevant to life in the 21st Century as they were in old Ben's day back in the 1700s.

Benjamin Franklin's 13 Virtues:

Virtue:	Ben's Meaning:	How we might interpret this today.
Temperance	Sat not to dullness nor drink to elevation.	All things in moderation.
Silence	Speak not but what may benefit others or yourself; avoid trifling conversation.	Listen more than you speak, you'll learn more, and gossip less.
Order	Let all your things have their places, let each part of your business have it's time.	Everything in it's right time and place – strive for efficiency.
Resolution	Resolve to perform what you ought, perform without fail what you resolve.	Have discipline to do what you say you will do.
Frugality	Make no expense but do good to others or yourself. Waste Nothing.	Spend less than you earn; *waste not, want not*.
Industry	Lose no time: always be employed in something useful; cut off all unnecessary actions.	Time is money – don't waste it. Make yourself useful.
Sincerity	Use no hurtful deceit; think innocently and justly, and if you speak, speak accordingly.	Think before speaking and speak honestly.
Justice	Wrong none by doing injuries or omitting the benefits that are your duty.	Do the right thing! What you do and say has consequences.
Moderation	Avoid extremes; forebear resenting	Balance, and seek moderation, not

	injuries so much as you think they deserve.	extremes in all parts of your life.
Cleanliness	Tolerate no uncleanliness in body, clothes, or habitation.	Be clean. Don't live like a pig or treat your home like a hovel.
Tranquillity	Be not disturbed at trifles, or accidents common or unavoidable.	Don't sweat the small stuff and focus on what you *can* control.
Chastity	Rarely use venery but for health of offspring, never to dullness, weakness, or the injury of your own or another's peace or reputation.	Be smart, careful, and consider your own and other's reputations regarding sexual activity.
Humility	Imitate Jesus and Socrates.	Be humble, not overconfident or arrogant.

Franklin was reported to have set each on a timetable of one week each to work on in his own character development, and rotated each seeing as it would be impossible to work on all at once in equal measure.

He was indeed a great man and worth of high praise in the many history books, and if he set out at such a young age to life his life this way, then he certainly benefited from having made such a decision to do so. As a side note – he also gave us three fantastic sayings that are worth repeating here:

Early to bed and early to rise makes a man healthy, wealthy, and wise.

Never leave that till tomorrow which you can do today.

Either write something worth reading or do something worth writing.

Some of the other definitions I found online for virtues related to the subject of character. For example, virtues are personal characteristics, or how a character is defined and shaped. Truthfulness, generosity, honesty, kindness and incorruptibility are also suggested as virtues in some dictionaries or as synonyms for virtues. Arguably as already noted in earlier chapters, some of these are also values.

I would like to point out however that core values rarely change, and virtues can be identified and fostered as part of one's character. And there-in lies the difference.

Character is of course different to values, and virtues, both of which add to one's character. Understanding these things together, are what we need to consider more when raising our children, so that there is less confusion about what all this means. This brings us to why we need to teach our children about Values.

10

Why we need to teach our kids about values

Imagine if we were able to explain easily to our younger generations the difference between value, Values, and Needs, and how they relate to each other? What being *out of or in* integrity actually means. How to more easily explain the difference in the needs and values of Narcissists, or people who need us to have firm boundaries around? Imagine their ability to work out if that friendship is really likely to be destructive based on their understanding of their own values from the start of it?

What about taking that one step further and having values form part of the questionnaire on a dating app, or knowing you need to be sure of each other's values before committing to a long-term relationship with a lover.?

How would your life be different today if you went back and reviewed those jobs, and those relationships that didn't go well for you, based on now understanding your own values better, as well as your needs? Imagine if before we engage in new friendships or employment opportunities we learned about our own and the others' values first, so we would know for sure if we're aligned for success.

Beliefs, imposters, and the rebels within us

If our kids learn about needs values, and core values then this will also play directly into their better understanding of how to deal with their beliefs, imposter syndrome and how or why they may develop a rebellious streak. A child of 10 with the belief that they are capable of achieving great things if they work hard, and that the value of what they do is worthwhile, then they have a better chance of success in life than if they start out with a belief that everything is hard work, and the odds are stacked against them. Let's take that first child and see what their positive belief relates to in terms of their values and needs.

Darius is bright, comes from a family who understands that he has a passion for computer games, and needs stimulation on a regular basis. He's not good at sitting still, fidgets a lot, and excels in sports. He has a dream of being a pro-rugby player.

- **His core values are fairness, discovery, and excellence.**

- **His core needs are adventure, winning, and being acknowledged.**

He's known to his family and friends as being the happy kid who steps in and helps the underdog, will not cheat at tests or games, and is reliable. School sports are where he achieves his best outcomes, and he's quick to defend his right to play in the top teams by being diligent about practice and demonstrates good leadership. He's often found doing the extra chores that get him bonus time with the coaches.

Because he's able to align his sports prowess with his values of excellence, fairness and his needs with winning and acknowledgement, it's easy for him to be on a trajectory of representative level sports, with potential for pro-am or professional opportunities later. His belief in his ability to do this is supported by his values. But – what if he gets to a new school or ends up in a new team where everyone has to be treated equally, regardless of skill and drive. What if his belief in his own ability to get him where he wants to go is dampened down by having that need of winning, and value of excellence compromised. What happens when his core value of fairness is supported (because okay, maybe every kid should have a chance to win the cup in equal measure) but at the expense of his needs for winning and acknowledgment. His ability to shine and operate from a place of excellence becomes impossible because the rules are no longer what he had believed were true for his life. In that instance, not only is his belief in the possibilities of becoming a superstar athlete diminished, but when he does have those times of being outstanding, an imposter sits on his shoulder and reminds him that he needs to let others win too. His imposter syndrome will argue with his values about his right to shine. Depending on how long he's allowed to shine and thrive as a junior star on a winning team will depend on how much of a rebel streak he's likely to have. He will either shine brightly, or shimmer and fade, and may always feel slightly out of integrity when it comes to winning, achieving, and being acknowledged. If he is picked up and nurtured towards that star status again then his values and needs are met and his belief in himself with every win will be reinforced.

Another child – Katie, has the ability to write beautiful stories. She also likes to read them out-loud and has a quirky sense of humor to go with these skills. She loves to entertain and inspire people to be happy.

Her Core Values are: Kindness, Humor, Imagination

Her Core Needs are: Energy, Creativity, To Share

Her stories are appreciated by her classmates, friends and her teachers. She has a talent for writing, and so is given the opportunity to explore poetry which she decides she's not really into, but comedy sketches are more her thing. So, as she develops in this area, she's tested by being put into the school plays to perform some of her work. Someone "boos" from the audience, when she forgets a line. She also gets a letter of rejection from a childrens' publishing competition the next day. She freezes and decides to stop sharing her work. Her two core values of kindness and humor have been directly attacked and it's enough to put her into a crisis of confidence.

Maybe she's not funny, or creative enough, and she definitely doesn't want to share her creativity anymore. Maybe being creative is not even a good idea... she instead turns her attention the following year into more science-based subjects. Her imposter syndrome fuels her belief in the idea that she's not funny and lacks talent in the areas she's actually very good at, but her negative beliefs have overridden her values and needs. One day someone will remind her that her core driver of imagination and kindness is also contained in the need to create and share. Her kindness to others stops short of being kind to herself until she learns her core values and needs are not being met. She finally returns to writing comedy for TV.

If kids were tested for their values and needs and then encouraged based on these, their ongoing beliefs in their abilities to navigate their futures would be so much easier. Their parents and teachers would also be better able to see when issues such as lack of self-esteem was central to a values or needs integrity issue.

What might the world look like if we learned these things early?

11

Relationship values

Ok, Confession time – I nearly put this book to bed before adding this vital chapter. Then it occurred to me that this critical section was missing – how to navigate our close personal relationships based on our core values. Because without our understanding how to do this, many of us will forever be stuck in lost perspectives, cross purposes, and misalignment with our loved ones.

I have been heard on more than one occasion suggesting that before any couple gets into commitment mode, they need to spend half a day in the classroom doing three tests:

1) Love languages – so that they know how best to give and receive love through the concepts of touch, words of affirmation, gifts, acts of service, and time spent together. If you have not explored this with your partner, regardless of how long you've been together I

highly recommend starting with Gary Chapman's book – The Five Languages of Love[1].

2) Personality profiles, so you can work out how to engage in productive combat when you're not seeing eye to eye. Learning that one of you is a detail oriented, ultra tidy, list making, well organized, neat freak before you move in with a fly-by-the-seat-of-her-pants type who can't scramble eggs without half destroying the kitchen is a great idea, because you're going to need a strategy to cope with each other, and fast to survive a long term relationship.

3) Values and needs analysis – so you know whether you are aligned with each other's wants, needs, and drivers.

When it comes to core values in a relationship, it's important to know that even if they are not aligned – i.e. one of you might be a risk taking adventurer and the other more about discovery and security – there needs to be something well understood between you that helps determine what kinds of holidays you'll take, how you'll raise the children or fur babies, and how you'll live through those teen years with your kids.

---

[1] The Five Languages of Love. Gary Chapman 2001, Northcote Publishing – A best seller for 20 years!

Let's consider this. Jade and Bob are madly in love and ready to take that giant leap of faith and have a baby together. They've been living together for a couple of years and still arguably in the honeymoon phase of their relationship. In their thirties, they don't want to wait too much longer to start a family, so that's really all there is to it they think. After all, they have good jobs, stable home life, and a bit of a long plan to buy a house in the country and travel more one day. But in completing their values exercise they discover that:

Jade is a teacher and actually quite adventurous, driven by core values of discovery, privacy, and improvement – and long term sees herself as being self-employed, traveling even while their children are young, maybe living in Europe for a few years, and teaching their children to be independent, curious and free spirited.

Rob's core values are nurturing, family, surety, and fairness. His work as a nurse is one that fits him perfectly, and although he could support Jade's vision as a teacher who travels and explores the world more, his long-term reality is more likely to be that they take holidays to fairly sensible places, raise the family and then set off on a bit more adventure, *maybe*.

Unless they really understand their respective values and learn to support each other at that level, they are likely to find one has maybe outgrown or outpaced the other in where they want ultimately to be. The early days of their relationship mean they each are likely to compromise some of their values in order to please the other.

Communication styles are the other big issues that come up with values in relationships. One might be very big on communication, and the other might be more reserved and private. Having open conversations about the most important parts of their relationships will prove challenging if they can't openly discuss things like money, sex, health, and other people. If one is driven by fairness as a core value, and the other is driven by privacy, their potential for disharmony in these critical areas is high.

Imagine this scenario. Jade wants them to share a bank account for *all* their savings after she gets pregnant because that seems fair, she's having the baby, and he's going to support them as a family because that's what they have agreed to do. Rob's always been great with money and has saved a lot more than Jade has over the years and feels there should be some firm conversations about equity and fairness, but Jade is quite private about money (and all things really) and doesn't really want to do that. It's not just a bad past experience with other partners, or warnings from friends about this, it's also part of both their values that drives their innermost feelings about this.

Sex is also an issue where open conversation and their respective values of privacy and discovery and improvement are guiding Jade to want to be private, but also keep on improving their sex lives over the years, but Rob's values of family and surety, complicate matters because he likes things to be somewhat predictable and puts family needs ahead of their personal time as a couple. Again, conversations about this critical area are complex because they are governed by quite diverse values, but they don't really understand that aspect of their relationship.

Here's the solution.

By understanding each other's values, they are at least likely to know what is triggering the other to behave in certain ways. How a very supportive person might need to give or receive support and encouragement must be understood by their partner who in turn might have core values relating to risk, and a need for freedom and independence.

Values are promoters of 'confidence in communication' within relationships.

This also extends to friendships. If you have a friend who does not align with your values of support and encouragement, and you're about to win a major award, you might feel a little cheated by their relative casualness about it. A friend who wants to honor their value of freedom by never committing to a firm time to do something together might really make you feel misaligned in the core value you have of structure or perfection.

***

I recommend that before you move into together, start a family, or go traveling as a couple you work out your intentions, but also get to know and fully understand your own and each other's core values and needs. Take time out for a couple of hours to work through the same personal values and needs exercise in chapter five and spend time talking about what your values means to you both as individuals and as a couple. See if you feel it changes anything, and if not, does it mean you need to have clarity around your Plan B when something is not aligning in the future.

This exercise could be the thing that saves many arguments, and misunderstandings, and also makes anniversaries, celebrations and unity between you mean even more meaningful.

Part Two:

Values in Business

12

Company values

Two of my previous books on marketing have each featured a chapter about the ideal of having business values, so that whatever marketing is undertaken, fits within that and aligns with the brand. The reality of working within your brand values for everything from Recruitment, Marketing, and Defining Your Purpose cannot be underestimated. First, you need to go through understanding what your company values are. Some examples of big brand's values might surprise you.

McDonald's values back in the early days were focused on cleanliness, family, and value for money, as well as efficiency. Think about that for a moment – by having cleanliness as one of its core values it appealed to mothers as being a safe place to have the kids eat and play, and that included the bathroom visits. As a McDonalds crew member back in 1990 I experienced first-hand some training around not only efficiency rules but also cleaning that made it abundantly clear that cleanliness was one of their core values. It was also safe for Moms to take one child to the bathroom and be pretty certain the older kids would be casually watched over by staff for anyone making someone feel uncomfortable in that situation. That's just how it was done then – and we employees knew that if someone asked for help in such a situation it was ok to step up by letting the manager know that someone needed help wrangling three kids by a single mum.

Virgin was always known for fun, value for money and a fresh attitude to doing things that pushed the boundaries of old traditional business methods. One of my first flights on a Virgin plane I experienced their commitment to a fun value by the way the entire plane was encouraged to sing happy birthday to a 10-year-old passenger and the safety demonstration being a little "out there" with references to hidden cameras in the toilets in case the smoke detectors weren't working.

You can generally sit and work out what many company values are by just thinking about how they demonstrate those values. Companies like Chrysler (Jeep) bring to mind rugged outdoors, tough. BMW make you think about luxury, quality, refinement. But here's a list[2] that I hope you reflect on as you read this next part.

---

[2] https://www.achievers.com/blog/company-core-value-examples/

- ***Google*** is about Excellence, Democracy Information, and Speed
- ***Kellogg's*** is about Accountability, Humility, Results, and Simplicity
- ***Olympus*** is about Unity, Agility, the long-term view, and Empathy

Olympus

Olympus Australia is a subsidiary of Olympus Corporation and is responsible for marketing and distribution of Olympus' line of innovative products to medial (media?), consumer and scientific businesses in Australia and New Zealand. Olympus's goal is to make people's lives healthier, safer and more fulfilling by practicing and living their core values.

- Unity: we are strongest when we work together as a team.
- Integrity: we are trustworthy and act in good faith.
- Empathy: we care about all of our stakeholders.
- Long-Term View: we look beyond the present to deliver future value.
- Agility: we challenge the status quo with open minds, focus, and speed.

My view is that a couple of these should be in the 'that's a given' category but at least they think about these and demonstrate them as living values for the company.

Kellogg's

Kellogg's is a quintessential USA brand who state their six core values as representative of the type of employees they want to attract, the businesses they wish to work with, and the types of products they produce to fit consumers' needs.

- Integrity
- Accountability
- Passion
- Humility
- Simplicity
- Results

They don't seem to have a list of what each of these means to them. But it's a nice list.

Google

Everyone in the world has heard of Google – it's ranked as of the top three most recognized brands in the world. Such an influential business needs killer corporate values, and Google does not disappoint. They refer to their values as 'the ten things we know to be true', and were originally written when Google was only a few years old.

1) Focus on the user and all else will follow.
2) It's best to do one thing, really, really well.
3) Fast is better than slow.
4) Democracy on the web works.
5) You don't need to be at your desk to need an answer.
6) You can make money without doing evil.
7) There's always more information out there.
8) The need for information crosses all borders.
9) You can be serious without a suit.
10) Great just isn't good enough.

Google has a corresponding paragraph fully explaining each of these tenets in detail. It is evident that Google takes their values extremely seriously and holds their employees to the highest standards. Google also mentions that they revisit their values to ensure that they are still in keeping with the company's goals and mission. They've done so multiple times since these were first written.

How can companies work out their company values?

First you need to identify what your values and core values are, and what the value proposition you offer customers is – based on what they most need, desire, fear. Decide then how you will most easily solve or deliver that product or service for them, at a price that is mutually agreeable. Then you have a business you can construct on those values.

One way to do this is simply to go back to Chapter 4 and do the Values test again, perhaps ensuring that several of your stakeholders also follow the same process and then work out between you all a consensus based on the same or similar values you share Let's say there are eight people and they all have core values that are similar but you still need to narrow that down a list to a workable set of four. In this case you might run that exercise again to pit the top eight against each other. For a new start up, this is an easy option.

Mission to Mars

I was interested in a concept for exploring company values a few years ago that talked about the Mission to Mars theory. The way this was presented to me was that if you had to choose four people from your business to go to Mars and create a new version of your current best version of your business, then who would they be, what made them the best candidates, and what were their common traits that made them ideal for the role?

From there, I could see an easy way to identify what each person's individual and then shared values were, so that you could easily take those and grid them up as mentioned in the last chapter and isolate those values down into being the company's core values.

This has worked in principle for me as a coach and consultant a number of times as I've worked with clients to help identify the collective values of a team. And while I've also heard of similar processes, the original company that introduced that concept to me has long since ceased to trade. I understand that the original version of this was developed by Verne Harnish, author of Mastering the Rockefeller Habits[3]. If you have a mix of great people in your business who might be reflective of the best of the company overall, take some time to consider what their personal values are, and then what they all have in common.

From there, work through the same process as outlined so far and narrow down what could be determined as the top 4-5 core values of your business.

If all the people in your company (or at least a reasonable cross section of management and non-management) were to work this out together you'd get a very good understanding of what the values are, and also how to then apply those values as part of the new leadership team.

Let's explore that further.

---

[3] Mastering the Rockefeller Habits, Verne Harnish, Gazelles, 2002

The cross section of people selected for this Mission to Mars might include the following:

Name/Position	Jamie/PA to the CEO	Mel/Maintenance Manager	Sigmund/Sales Manager	Nick/Production Supervisor
Values	<u>Efficiency</u> <u>Helpfulness</u> <u>Security</u> Preparedness	Ingenuity <u>Curiosity</u> <u>Helpfulness</u> Creativity	Encouragement <u>Security</u> Connection Improvement	<u>Efficiency</u> Discernment <u>Curiosity</u> <u>Helpfulness</u>

You can see that the common values shared between them are:

- Efficiency
- Helpfulness
- Security
- Curiosity

As a group of leaders for the next version of the company, these would be the core values you'd want to be sure were articulated for customers and any other stakeholders through marketing, recruitment, and management decisions.

How that might look:

The Value	The Benefit (this means that...)
We are efficient	We will get the job done within the stated and agreed timeframes.
Our Helpfulness	Ensures that you will be guided towards making the best decisions based on the outcomes you require, using all our resourcefulness and understanding of what you are seeking to achieve.
Security is important to us	So that means we understand your need to know your deposit is safe/your information is well protected...
We are curious	We'll always ask for feedback to ensure we are at the front of the industry trends and understanding of our customer's wants and needs. That way we know how best to continually improve our products and services.

When engaging new people to join a company like this, seeking a good fit of values that are reflected in these core values is key to your success. If you want people who are also efficient, helpful, and security minded you'll get them. But if you end up with Jonny whose values are *Diligence, Sensuality, Bliss, and Adventure,* they may not fit quite so well as Sally whose values are *Fostering, Compassion, Investigate,* and *Surety*. Because the values of *Investigative* and *Surety* align well with *Curiosity* and *Security*. And for a sales position working with Sigmund whose core value is also *Encouragement, Fostering* is another good alignment.

13

Displaying and living your brand values

I called into a housing company last week to investigate some building options. They are a high-tech build-on-site operation who then truck and crane the finished cottages or small simple shaped dwellings to where they are intended to become homes or vacation rentals.

As I wandered about the show home – which was lovely, as expected, I noticed that they had three frames on the wall stating their mission, vision, and Core Values. I read with interest that their values included Respect, Honesty, Integrity, and Quality. *Mmmn….* So that didn't really tell me anything of real significance. Except that they were regular normal people who thought I might value as a potential customer that they had at least thought a little about this, or maybe invested in a few books or a business coach who could walk them through a standard exercise on the subject.

Their mission was to build a quality future exceeding the expectations of customers, shareholders and stakeholders. *Nice but terribly vague.*

Their vision was specified as wanting to be the best housing company in the region.

Sadly, this is where they lost me as a potentially excited customer. Now, I might return, because the quality was nice, and the prices okay, but not because I was in any way buying into their vision, mission, or aligned with their values.

As Simon Sinek, author of *Start With Why*[4] says, values are nouns. You need to get to the WHY. And the How is just *how* you do what you do. But people don't buy from you because of what you do, they buy because of why you do it. And values are very closely associated with those whys, and these are VERBS. *Yet another V word.*

Let me give you a great example:

At a lovely South Pacific resort, the original gazillionaire founder was honoured with a brief speech one day, by someone who was associated with one of his many companies, and well familiar with this resort. It was pointed out that their benevolent founder had in his lifetime given much to charity, universities, and even had places of interest named after him.

---

[4] Start With Why, Simon Sinek, Penguin 2011

He also apparently had a great vision, to create this wonderful resort facility.

The problem was, he gave this brief but in-depth speech about things well out of reach of nearly every person there. The housemaids, grounds-people, maintenance men, and hospitality workers were likely to never be able to afford to stay at such a place as their guests and having places named after their founder in other countries did not mean anything to any of those present either. The vision was complete – the palace on the hill existed. But was there anything more?

The reality is that everyone turned up for their pay checks, not because they believed in what they were doing, or had a passion for creating something bigger than they individually could relate to.

And that's a sad reality for most companies around the world. There are a million books on leadership available, and if you do a search for the word on LinkedIn you'll find more than 100,000 options to click through to, but there is an astounding shortage of leadership in the world right now. So, it's not about a lack of knowledge available for people to master the art of leadership. I believe that a lack of understanding about Value, Values, Core Values and the needs that these connect to is the reason we are missing a few good Nelson Mandelas, Mahatma Ghandis, and William Wallace types in the 21st century so far.

What does your brand mean?

High Quality. Budget Deals. A Fair Deal. More Value for Money. Image. Great Service. Fun. Accountability.

These are just a few examples of how companies may position themselves and want to be perceived by their customers.

4WD luxury vehicle owners possibly ski or hunt, wear top of the line clothing, and expect to travel in comfort and style, and to look good. So faced with deciding on two types of promotional sports bags as a gift-with-purchase of a $100,000 vehicle, some of the deciding factors might be:

Brand Values =	Rugged	Masculine	Stylish	Expensive Looking	Hard Wearing
Leather Bag	✓	✓		✓	✓
Canvas Bag	✓	✓	✓		

Factors such as top stitching, brass rivets, extra pockets might all add to the value of both bags, but one will probably represent your brand values more effectively than the other –

in this case, a leather bag may be presumed to be harder wearing than its canvas equivalent.

Another example could be a budget stationery company, who's brand values are dependable, low cost, good quality, wide range, customer satisfaction.

If considering two different styles of pen, one we'll call *Pen A* has been around for generations, a well-known hard-working brand that is known to work on lots of surfaces, is very low cost and available in 40 combination colours. The other one, *Pen B*, is also plastic, new to the market, has a gold trim, and is a little flashy looking, and is available in 6 colours. Chances are the gold will wear off after a while, but it may still be a pen style that people will perceive as being more expensive, and therefore better value.

In short – both are good quality, and will suit the company image, but when checking them against the brand values – one will be more suitable than the other for this particular company.

Brand Values =	Customer Service	Dependability	Low Cost	Wide Range	Good Quality
Item A		✓	✓	✓	✓
Item B			✓		✓

Item A is more suitable for this company to use as it rates better with more of its brand values.

Don't compromise your brand values; recognise them, publish them, and refer to them when making buying decisions about any promotional product that carries your brand.

14

Recruitment and company values

Imagine for a moment the challenges of finding and keeping great employees being dramatically simplified. Would you be smiling at the thought of that? Sound like a dream come true? It could be far more than just fantasy if you bring the concept of values and needs into the equation.

Many recruiters use psychology tools such as DISC profiling as part of their recruitment process now. As a trained DISC user myself I know that I've found this to be invaluable in terms of insights when onboarding clients, establishing business and even personal relationships. But the use of Values is another level again when it comes to surrounding yourself with the best people. I'm a big fan of Brad Smart's book *Top Grading*[5]. He talks all about the importance of getting the right fit with regards to recruitment. As he points out: *"Recruit for Fit, the skills are almost an additional bonus if*

---

[5] Top Grading Revised Edition 2012, Brad Smart, Published by Portfolio

you get the fit right. And you can always teach additional skills." Again, I believe this is more about values and needs than even psychology – I have to state here again that I am not a psychologist. I'm sure there are many who might also disagree with me on this point, but here's the thing. If you have common values, then your ability to understand each other with empathy is enhanced considerably.

Let's explore how this works in reality.

Joseph is seeking a new middle manager with HR skills to join his construction company. There are 22 employees, mostly men on the work crews, and women in the office. He wants to balance out the testosterone a little with a man in the office but knows he can't advertise for that. It's illegal to discriminate, but what he does know is that the family values they have in ABC Construction is a big deal to all the employees, and so the ideal scenario is to get an older man who also has similar family-based values. The other core values for this company are sharing, excellence, and quality.

The criterion for applicants is that they must be family oriented, willing to work in a team which shares information and skills, and focused on helping their company to deliver on its promise of quality homes to young families. The successful applicant must also have firm understanding of current HR legislation for the construction industry and good attention to detail.

The advert goes out, and the replies come in. Applicants who have not indicated they can deliver on the skills indicated of human resources, recruitment, legal understanding of the job, and have graduated within the last five years are set aside. Three candidates stand out as being of potential interest – two men aged 50+, and one woman in her forties. Finding that all have teenage children is a bonus, and that all have the similar or same work skills makes the initial selection process quite difficult. All candidates seem 'really nice'.

Joseph asks each candidate to complete a DISC profile and to complete a Values and Needs exercise similar to the one outlined in this book.

Here's how the candidates look by the time they have gone through this additional process.

Ann – 46, married 18 years, twins in high school, loves hiking, photography and skiing holidays in the winter.	Barry – 51, lives with his partner, 2 sets of kids – aged 12-21, loves sailing, wine tours, and amateur theatre.	Peter – 53, second marriage, children in university, one grandchild, loves hanging out with his family, volunteers for scouts, and plays piano in a jazz band.
DISC profile shows High C for compliance, and S for stable.	DISC profile shows High C for compliance, and D for Drive	DISC profile shows High S for Stable, and I for Influence – i.e. very outgoing.
Values: Achievement, Risk, Mastery, Helpfulness **Needs:** Appreciation, for things to be aesthetically pleasing, and friendship.	**Values:** Connection, communication, fairness, sharing **Needs:** Community, stability and security.	**Values:** Knowledge, sensitivity, communication **Needs:** Fun, certainty and to be good at things.

All three candidates on paper might be ideal.

- Ann loves to get out and explore and have some adventure, and also evidently has a keen eye for detail.
- Peter is also outgoing, friendly, and likes to do things well, and is a dedicated family man, stable and reliable.
- But Barry has an understanding of blended families, the value of communication and connection and sharing. He also needs stability and security – and that's in line with what ABC Construction's values are also reflective of.

Would you have a different view based only on the DISC Profiles?

If you can address what someone's needs are, and identify and align with an employee's values, then you have a much clearer insight into what will motivate or de-motivate good people.

Let's look at another version of this:

A school with children aged 5 – 12 is seeking a librarian. The school is a special place for children often requiring higher input for special needs, at the very super bright end of the spectrum. Many of the children are also highly strung, easily bored, and smart enough to run rings around their teachers if given the chance to do so. The school is very focused on preparing children to possibly start university at a younger than usual age, and most of the students are also very creative. The school puts out an advertisement seeking the following:

A librarian who is gifted academically, but also loves the power of story to demonstrate life lessons. Must understand the EXCY System we use for cataloguing, but also be kind natured, firm in attitude and really love to learn.

Two candidates stand out as being ideally suited to the job:

Suni – 34, Single, well-traveled, tri-lingual, has just purchased a house to be near her family, runs marathons, studies comedy and history, and brews her own ginger beer.	Jason – 42, Married with one 4 year old son, is a former teacher of music, passionate about books and technology, and is writing a young adult fantasy series he hopes to publish one day.
DISC profile shows high I for Influence and S for stable.	DISC profile shows high S for Stable and C for compliance

Values: Achievement, Helpfulness, Fun Needs: Appreciation, adventure, and to improve.	Values: Knowledge, Fun, Perfection Needs: Things to be correct, punctuality, and to learn new things.,

If your special school for gifted children had values of achievement, knowledge, and community, which of these candidates would you hire?

In this instance either Suni or Jason would be potentially a good fit, and so there is no right answer, but you can see how it is much easier to distinguish more of what either would bring to the role than simply stopping at what their academic qualifications and work experience might be from their resume and application.

15

Leadership and values

As I briefly highlighted in chapter 11, Simon Sinek says: *"People don't buy what you do, they buy why you do it."* When it comes to leadership, understanding and articulating your 'why' is what leadership is all about. It's not managing people to fall into line or do the tasks well as laid out by the management team. It's about inspiring people to follow you in your endeavor to build something, make a change, or create a new something.

Sinek gives the example of two men who are bricklayers, both working long backbreaking hours for little financial reward. One sees himself as a bricklayer building a wall. The other sees himself as contributing to the creation of a church where people will meet and connect. Which one is working for a great leader?

You see, when people know why they are doing something, 'the what' is the part about getting it done, and 'the how' is about the implementation of the skills and resources required to get it done. But 'the why' is the purpose. It's the reason for people to get up every day and get busy doing the how.

I was recently at a big day out for a company who wanted to honor their employees for their hard work and provide a lunch and a bonus day off. A couple of speeches were made by two long standing employees who had been part of the company 22 years ago when it was first launched. The founder had passed away only a few days earlier, at a great age, and was spoken about warmly by these two long standing employees. "He was a kind man, a good man, and a generous man", they said. "He had a dream to build this place and realized that dream." But they focused on the achievements of the man, including a very large donation of artwork to the country's national gallery. They did not talk about what the future looked like for the next generation of owners – his sons – and they did not inspire the continuation of a dream about a place were people could go and do the things the place was designed to do. It matters not in this example what that is, only that this is unfortunately a typical eulogy style that does not plant the seeds, nor water the young plants of inspiration for everyone to remain excited about turning up for work each day.

It's also not the kind of leadership that gets into the hearts of everyone, because there is a strong sense of purpose. The employees of that company are not likely to ever see that donation of art so generously donated to the country. For a start it will take years for the cataloguing and sorting of it, and then it will mostly be traded with other countries' galleries for show. Not to mention people working on the landscaping, and cleaning aspects of the company are arguably less likely to know a Monet from a Picasso piece of art anyway.

However, in stark contrast, if the direction of the company was talked about in relation to their values, the levels of inspiration might have been quite different by the end of that lunch. Their values – as posted up in the staff room, are teamwork, being service oriented, and having a can-do attitude.

One of the things about Values, is that *you have to own your own values*. For example, one of their values is written as **Teamwork: 'I am caring, flexible and respectful'**. But should that not be just a 'given' for any team member? And if your own core values are not specifically those things, then this is not a value, it's an affirmation.

You can't write affirmations as a value and hope that your employees all get that.

You also can't write a set of values and hope that as a leader, your managers and staff all embrace your own values.

Unless you hire people who fit within those values as part of your recruitment strategy.

The vision – also posted up on the staffroom wall, states that: [this company] *will create moments worth sharing and create experiences to which our guests can hardly wait to return to.*

Does that inspire people working on minimum wage to get up and get to work every day?

Let's dial this back a bit ...

For a leader to inspire people, they need to know what the leader's values are. And how those values are akin to the purpose of the company. Let's take another look at Richard Branson. He lives his values, and it's clear to see that his laid-back jersey/barefoot/canalboat lifestyle as Virgin was being created in the early days juxtaposed fun with efficiency and better value service for customers. That has not changed. Sure, it may have been well tested at times, but The Virgin brand is arguably still about fun, efficiency and better value service for customers than what the opposition offers. It's also always been about pushing boundaries, innovation, and thinking better about what's possible.

Apple is still about breaking the status quo of 'boring' in creative and dynamic tools to make people's lives better.

- Marketing is about Values.
- Recruitment is about Values.
- Leadership is about Values.

People want to be able to follow leadership that reflects values and inspires through a vision to articulate those values.

I believe Vision and Values are closely aligned for most leaders. If they know their values, and they are working in an organization (even if not their own) that allows them to reflect shared values, then the ability to articulate a vision is unbelievably powerful. And that's what people buy into. The vision supported by the values of the leadership.

And that brings us to passion!

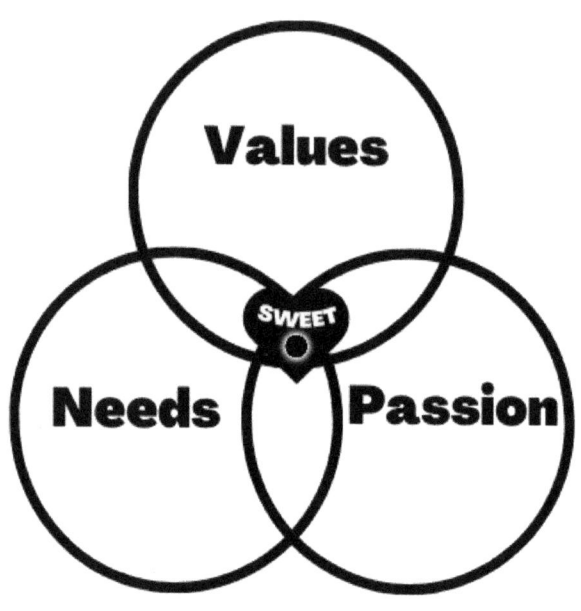

That P Word

Passion is not a V word, but it does belong in this book. Because when you intersect Passion with Values and Needs, then you have something BIG. In the center of this Venn-diagram is the sweet spot for all projects, companies, and individuals wanting to get clarity on who and what they are here to achieve in this life.

Passion is what enables you to harness your most burning desire, marry your personal values and needs and create something absolutely amazing with unstoppable energy. And to inspire others to join you on making that a reality.

If you want to create a business that sells a better widget or provides a better service to a clearly defined target market, your passion for that project will take you so far.

For Example:

Let's say you want to create a barbershop.

A barbershop for men aged 25-55

... who have survived or are working through a divorce

... and need to talk about their day

... to feel some personal caring and appreciation

... to feel confident about the potential first date again

... to feel like they can talk to that girl or guy at the next table

... to walk out knowing they paid well for a sympathetic ear and a kind word

And your passion is primarily to help deeply wounded men who are battling for their rights to be fathers and taken seriously in their next relationship. Men who maybe feel a bit battle scarred and need a bit of a tidy up and to get ready for their next foray into dating. Hey, women get makeovers, so why not the same for men, right?

Your own values are compassion, curiosity, helpfulness, and attractiveness. Your vision is to have more mid-life men to have more successful second relationships. You're only going to hire people who also want that same vision, and to contribute towards a happier population of men who date, marry, and raise great kids. Keeping it simple, you ensure that your values are reflected and aligned in what you do, the people you hire, and the services that form part of your brand.

You can extrapolate that concept out to any kind of business.

16

Summary

In finishing up this book it's very important to note one thing. This is about how to live and work better. By knowing your values, and your needs, and where they intersect, you'll improve your life, simply because you'll understand where and how things are out of balance, and therefore out of integrity for you.

You personally!

Remember that your core values, general values, needs and passions are different to everyone else's. But there are alignment opportunities everywhere. In your friendships, with colleagues, work opportunities, relationships, families… yes, everywhere. In order to recognize that alignment, you must know what your own needs and values are.

There is another part to getting your life working for you. Taking the time to think about and work in the following four areas will also help you.

You have four key areas of your life that you have total control over, and yet many of us fail to recognize this, or act on making these a priority. Understanding your needs and your values is critical, but when you also add in your attitude towards these four areas, and make some new habit-forming decisions about them, you'll notice some extraordinary changes in your life too.

How you Move.

How you move, means stretching, walking, exercising, so that you feel comfortable in your own body. It will help you manage pain, by noticing where and how your body reacts to all kinds of stimuli, so get familiar with your own body and take charge over how you move it.

Honor your need to move your body in a way that is right for you personally. Get massages to ensure your fascia is supple and your muscles are moving as they should be. Deep tissue massage is also regenerative for your body in so many ways.

How you sleep.

When you sleep well, and that means 6-8 hours of *quality* sleep, you can move better, and function better in most circumstances. Tiredness means you are more likely to have challenges with honoring your needs and your values. Because being tired makes it easy to get lazy and then 'go with the flow Jo' becomes an easy mantra to live by. But when you are alert, well rested, and ready for the day ahead – every day - your ability to recognize when you are in or out of integrity throughout the day is improved. So, honor your need to sleep.

Then when or if you have a late night, your sleep bank will ensure your overall quality of sleep is barely challenged within the week. Consider your own needs regarding reading, screen or TV time, how you choose to prepare for bed, and for sleep, and what you have in your sleep space that helps you. Some people like to use essential oils, have a bath, or a cup of calming tea too. Do what works for you. But make this a regular habit.

How you Breathe.

Breathing is something that we mostly don't consider in terms of learning how to do it well. But if you shallow breathe – i.e. through your chest – it affects your oxygen flow throughout your body. It can also make you more tired and affect how well you talk if you need to talk beyond short sentences at any time. Learn to breathe from your diaphragm, so your lungs fill, and you have control over your inhale and exhale of oxygen into your body. Managing your ability to breathe deeply and control the flow of air passing through your body and through your throat, means you can deliver information more succinctly, without your voice frying (crackling) or getting tired.

So, honor your ability to breathe well. If you talk as part of your daily work, then invest in some voice lessons so you learn to breathe as you speak so you are fresher and more authoritative when speaking. Your ability to breathe deeply can help you sleep better and move better too.

How you Think

You have the ability to manage your thoughts, but it can take practice to get to the point of doing this easily. Affirmations can help you focus on positive thoughts and conditioning your mind to become more focused on seeing the good versus the negative in situations or circumstances every day. As Robin Sharma said in his best-selling book *The Monk Who Sold His Ferrari*,[6] "when you form the habit of searching for the positive in every obstacle or adversity, your life will move into its highest dimensions."

The ability to see things from different perspectives is a learned thing. Reading great books, meditating, and learning

---

[6] The Monk Who Sold His Ferrari – Robin Sharma, HarperOne 1999

to slow your thoughts down can be life changing on its own. But combined with honoring your need to Move, Sleep, Breathe and Think better as daily habits, you will find these support your life when lived in the integrity of honoring your needs and your values.

A brief word on Meditation

This is not about learning to stop the monkey mind, but about allowing the thought processes in your mind to flow differently. Learning to say the right things to yourself when a negative thought invades your mind is a different thing. That's about ensuring that you take charge of how you manage self-doubt, imposter syndrome, and negative thinking by replacing the thought with a simple command to 'move on' or replace it with a more positive one.

There are lots of books about Moving, Sleeping, Breathing and Thinking better. This is not a book about those and I'm not going to devote a whole chapter to promoting ways to do these things.

This is a book about That V Word – Values. Values and Needs, and how they relate to your ability to make decisions, understand what drives those decisions, and to trust in yourself when you do. But these four things will help you to recognize your alignment with those values and needs. So please honor them as part of your commitment to honoring your values and living them every day.

Resources and Tools

If you wish to download the full Values and Needs lists, the family values and the analysis grids, you will find these on my website, along with some additional bonus articles, resources, and tools that will be updated as they get thought about.

If you need additional help to navigate your way through determining your values and how they are presented and honored in your daily life, your company, or your family, please reach out for more information about any of the following:

- Coaching – personal and executive coaching options
- Company and Brand Values – workshop
- Book Dixie Carlton to speak at your next event.

Access your copy of That Sex Book. This is the other book in the Taboo Conversations series.

Simply go to:

www.dixiecarlton.com/ThatVWord

Acknowledgements

Some special people went into helping me to finesse and finish this book. A big thanks to my Beta readers, Bronwyn Reid, Tania Roberts, Steph Weldon, and Adam Walsh.

To Daniela Catucci for yet another fabulous cover design and Lindsey Dawson and Geoff Taylor for feedback and proofing,

To my sons Nix and Alex for their feedback and extraordinary conversations about values and parenting. As my two 'all time favorite guinea pigs' too, you made it so easy to learn and develop this material over the years. And to Hannah and Stacey for helping our family to continue to live in integrity of our values and the many amazing conversations had about this around coffee pots and desserts.

Thank you.

Other books by Dixie Maria Carlton

Non-fiction:

In the Taboo conversations series:

- That Sex Book – How to talk about and get a hot sex life after 50

In the Authority Author's series:

- Start With the Draft – how to plan and write your first draft of a non-fiction book
- From Idea to Authority - write, publish and market a non-fiction book
- Authority Island – why some authors become authorities and others just write books.

Buying and Selling Old Stuff

Small Business Start -up Essentials

The Power of Promotional Products

To engage Dixie to speak at your next event please visit www.dixiecarlton.com/speaker-topics

About Dixie Maria Carlton

Dixie has been igniting and curating conversations with random strangers since she was a very small precocious red headed child. She has no fear of striking up a conversation with anyone, anytime, anywhere, learning new things from people she meets and asking tough questions. As a coach, trained by Coach U/Coach Inc back in the early '00s' she honed those skills further (than a few decades of sales and marketing had enabled her to do) in the art of conversation and turned her attention to writing books.

Values in her work as a coach, marketing, and publishing specialist have always been a critical connector for Dixie working with clients, and a particular area of interest since first being introduced to some of the concepts of 'living life on purpose' in her early coach training. She eloquently incorporates this into her writing and speaking, and personal life.

For More – including options for Coaching, Mentoring, Publishing, Consulting and Retreats, please visit:

www.dixiecarlton.com